HIGH-ACCESS HOME

HIGH-ACCESS HOME

DESIGN AND DECORATION FOR BARRIER-FREE LIVING

CHARLES A. RILEY II

RIZZOLI
NEW YORK

First published in the United States of America by
Rizzoli International Publications, Inc.
300 Park Avenue South
New York, NY 10010

LIBRARY OF CONGRESS CATALOGING-IN-PUBLICATION DATA
Riley, Charles A.
     High-Access Home : design and decoration for barrier-free living
  Charles A. Riley, II.
        p.   cm.
Includes index.
ISBN 0-8478-2213-3
1. Architecture and the physically handicapped. 2. Dwellings-
-Access for the physically handicapped.   I. Title.
NA2545.P5R53   1999
720'.87—dc21   99-14404
                                                               CIP

DESIGNED BY RENATO STANISIC

Printed in Singapore

Front cover: clockwise from upper left, multi-level kitchen counters, photography by Barry Halkin,
courtesy DuPont Corian ®; tea kettle by OXO, Vanessa Sica, Mari Ando, Scott Bolden, Smart Design,
photography by ClausNY Inc. P. Medilek; Real Life Design Kitchen by General Electric, Louisville, KY,
designer, Mary Jo Peterson; Copco chopper and bowl set, Annie Brekenfeld, Smart Design, photography by
ClausNY, Inc. P. Medilek

Listen, there's a hell of a good universe next door.

—e.e. cummings

Contents

1

SHEER ELEGANCE

2

RIGHT FROM THE START

3

BACK TO THE FUTURE

4

TOWARD ACCESSIBILITY-ROOM BY ROOM

Acknowledgments

The not-so-small world of Universal Design is replete with individuals and organizations deeply committed to making all our lives easier through smart thinking on the built environment, and this book is an homage to their dedication and ingenuity. Among the vanguard to whom we owe our thanks, after the example of the late Ron Mace who coined the phrase "Universal Design," are Kim Beasley of the Paralyzed Veterans of America; George Covington, former White House adviser, author, and design consultant; Terry Moakley of the Eastern Paralyzed Veterans Association; Dianne Pilgrim, director of the Cooper-Hewitt National Design Museum; Allan Neumann, preservation architect; the late Marc Harrison, RISD professor of industrial design; Valerie Fletcher; and William Lebovich, architectural historian and photographer.

The leaders of the disability rights movement, with whom 54 million Americans place their trust, are also deserving of our gratitude, and they include Sara Brewster of Easter Seals, national office, General Mike Dugan of the National Multiple Sclerosis Society, Jerry Lewis of the Muscular Dystrophy Association, Bobby Muller of the Vietnam Veterans of America Foundation, Homer S. Townsend Jr. of the

Paralyzed Veterans of America, Tony Coelho of the President's Committee on the Employment of Disabilities, Dr. Richard Traum of the Achilles Track Club, and Michael Simonson of United Cerebral Palsy.

WE, the first lifestyle magazine for people with disabilities has used a bold palette to paint the vivid picture of Universal Design, and without the efforts of the devoted editorial and advisory team that created the magazine and made it a success, this book would not have come to light. I would like to thank in particular Chairman Jerome Belson, Publisher Dr. Cary Fields, and the entire *WE* family: Fran Ahders, Jane S. Van Ingen, Fred A. Eno, Rosemarie Blitchington, Carol Ann Burton, Matthew Belson, Nicole Bianco, Aaron Silberman, Nancy Isenberger, Eric Jackier, Olga Hill, Robert P. Bennett, Stephanie Hammerman, Henry Holden, Casey Martin, Dr. David McMullen, Jill Gray Rosser, James J. Weisman, Tom Whittaker, John M. Williams, Gordon C. Harper, Lori Frisher, Wilson Hulley, Dick Sheppard, Diane Fiorentino, Francesca Rosenberg, Bruce Robert Burton, Anthony Razza, and Nirdi Relis.

At Rizzoli, the keen editorial eye of Melissa Moyal has given the book the sharp focus that the subject deserves. Designer Renato Stanisic has met the daunting challenge of designing a satisfying book on design. Carole Sinclair of Sinclair Media was instrumental in bringing the project together, and it was realized thanks in part to research by Anita Dickhuth and Richard Seidel of Artemis Picture Research Group Inc.; Carol Dobson; Don Owens; and Andrew Ackers.

Bruce Hannah, co-curator of *Unlimited by Design* at the Cooper-Hewitt, and John Hurst of Ironmonger were quite generous with their resources and time. I would also like to thank Eugenie H. Devine of Centerbrook Architects and Planners, Essex, CT, for being so diligent in finding the slides for the House near New York and Evelyn Krasnow of Smart Design, Inc. for helping to make the cover look as wonderful as it does.

My heartfelt thanks as well to my long-suffering wife Liu Ke Ming, and to my family and friends, all of whom have had to wait endlessly for me to shut the laptop and return to the land of the living. Without that support, the writing simply never flows; with them behind me, it becomes a book.

Introduction: A Home for All Ages

Welcome to the home of the future—your future, that of your parents, or somebody you know and love. It offers an array of utterly ingenious conveniences for ease of living and safety. Surprisingly it is not some sleek, cyber-savvy construction in glass and stainless steel conceived by the mind of a futurist, although in some respects it is more similar to a posh push-button personal paradise than to any off-the-rack modern house of a decade ago. In some cases, these homes are the updated versions of modernism's former state-of-the-art devices, incorporating research that is targeted specifically toward minimizing the strength and effort needed to accomplish the most mundane of movements.

This future home, whose time is now, is neither fantasy nor fiction. Its foundation is a philosophy that represents the latest wave in thinking about what is and is not a "functional environment" for all ages, and particularly for an aging population.

From the moment you pull up in the car, this house in Chestnut Hill, MA offers a warm welcome, thanks in large part to the fact that there is not one step to negotiate on the way to the door.

Called Universal Design, it had its origins in the need for accessible or "barrier-free" living shared by 54 million Americans (one in every five) with disabilities. As its founders and early supporters soon realized, however, Universal Design offered a wide range of benefits to people of all ages and abilities, by creating an environment in which we all could feel more comfortable and at home. Think for a moment of the automatic garage door, which originated out of necessity for a client whose disability prevented him from lifting a heavy door. Now a staple of living for nearly all of us so-called "able-bodied" people as well as those with disabilities, it is but one of many examples of how Universal Design has raised the bar for home design of all kind.

Let the image of a gently sloping path to an invitingly wide front door with a handsome brass lever start you off. You pass into a wide, airy foyer, brightly lit at the touch of a pad, or lit automatically as the floor senses your presence. You move into the kitchen where countertops and cooktops are at adjustable heights, or turn to the bathroom—not the typical tight space with slippery floor and metal sills, but a spacious area where the shower is roll-in and accident proof, meaning you cannot trip or stub your toe on a step. You never reach for a light switch, or bend to get to an outlet. A range of remote controls, like the television clicker, can raise the shades on the windows, set a compact disk turning on the stereo, or flick on the screen and camera to let you know if the dog is at the back door.

Rethinking the home for accessibility means widening the hallways for better maneuverability in a wheelchair, as seen in the state-of-the-art, elegant home of the Schwartz family in Petaluma, CA.

Quality of life. Thoughtful, well-executed plans. Spaces designed for everyone, without regard for preconceived categories such as nondisabled or disabled, young or old, short or tall. These standards set by Universal Design make life easier for everyone in the home.

The Mission of Universal Design

Lifestyles change throughout the course of one's life, and the architect and builder of a home have to be sensitive to changing needs. Universal Design is nothing more than good design, smart design, sensitive design. Some of its principles have been around a long time; others are fresh off the drawing board. For families who have experienced mobility, hearing, or visual conditions that require modifications, they are necessities—for the other beneficiaries they are the unnoticed amenities that make all the difference.

At first glance a home designed according to the principles of Universal Design does not look any different from a traditional, well-designed home. Appearances are deceiving—many little improvements distinguish the home with a Universal Design as user-friendly. The connoisseur of Universal Design appreciates its invisibility as much as its functionality.

The seamlessness and subtlety of Universal Design is an important aspect of its philosophy. Home design and personal identity are closely linked. As people drive by a home with a conspicuous ramp shooting straight up the front walkway, or see tubular stainless-steel grab bars in a hallway that resemble a hospital or nursing home, they fall prey to their own fears of disease or disability. A design that makes these features obvious also has the capacity to make the person using them look and feel less capable. But the time has passed when a new home can be churned out to suit the "average" person, a young, able-bodied, six-foot-tall male. The light switches are too high, the electrical outlets too low, the doorknobs a nuisance.

The key to easy movement between floors is the installation of a residential elevator, which more and more architects are drawing into their plans for homes.

Sometimes ease of access
translates into a concept as
simple as allowing more space.
At the Schwartz home in
Petaluma, CA, the garage por-
tals, doorways, and walkways
are more generous, allowing
not only a wheelchair user but
everyone in the family more
room to get around.

The most dramatic recent example of the triumph of Universal Design is the kitchen project at Rhode Island School of Design, which offers high-tech solutions to common problems, such as shelves that are hard to reach or a cooktop that is too high. Now these things can be lowered at the touch of a keypad for easy reach from a wheelchair.

The problem is perpetuated, in part, with the accumulation of misguided design. Universal Design is more than an issue of aesthetics, economics, or academics for many people—it is a cause. As George Covington, former special assistant for disability to the vice-president of the United States and co-chair of the Universal Design Task Force of the President's Committee on Employment of People with Disabilities, comments, "Most of the elements in our society that define us as 'the disabled' are caused by poor design. If I cannot find a building's address because the numbers are tiny or artistically hidden, I am 'visually impaired.' If a friend of mine in a wheelchair blocks the narrow aisle in a grocery store or cannot get onto a sidewalk because there is no curb cut, my friend is 'mobility impaired.' In the past, designers have failed to realize that when a disability meets a barrier, it creates a handicap. A landscape architect, a designer of furniture, or a computer engineer is each a designer, no matter what their titles. A person who creates a bank or credit-card statement that can't be read or understood by millions is a designer. There is not a single aspect of our daily lives that is not affected by designers. Too often those creations throw up barriers that result in our being labeled 'the disabled.'"

For Covington, who has only 5 percent of his sight due to macular degeneration, the universal in Universal Design is nearly literal. He continues: "The object of Universal Design is to create a building or a product that can be used by the widest range of individuals possible. When it can be used independently by both someone who is eight years old and one who is eighty, then it hits the essence of Universal Design. By designing for as broad a market as possible, it is no longer 'special,' setting a certain consumer apart from everyone else. Universal Design at its best is seamless, almost invisible."

The true test of Universal Design is the creation of a home for a lifetime. It is not furnished from a hospital catalogue, and it needn't be prohibitively expensive even in the conversion. Nor should beauty and elegance be among the sacrifices made. The key to the process is the identification and elimination of barriers, many of them traditional.

It may come as a surprise to discover who is among the vanguard of those who live better thanks to Universal Design. Many of those who already live in the home

Universal Design, now a movement that helps everyone, began as the handiwork of Ron Mace and the Universal Design Excellence Project at North Carolina State University. Here we see his elegant plan for making an inaccessible, stepped doorway to a home, above, into an easily negotiated and aesthetically pleasing barrier-free entrance.

of the future are themselves household names, including actor Christopher Reeve, newsman John Hockenberry, musician Itzhak Perlman, White House counsel Charles Ruff, and Senator Max Cleland. Living with a disability, and living well, they have turned the principles of Universal Design to their fullest advantage.

Laying Down the Rules

Universal Design grew up in the 1970s at the Center for Accessible Housing at North Carolina State University. Its first guru was Ron Mace, the director of the Center and a wheelchair user, following a bout with polio, since childhood. Mace, who died in 1998, established the building codes for accessibility that have been adopted by many states. His goal was to build to suit the entire life span of clients, not just to appeal to the present. The houses that Mace created would have fit inconspicuously into any neighborhood. The universal features are generally standard building products that have been placed differently. In addition, the level walks and the wider doorways, which became a signature of this type of design, made accessibility easier not just for wheelchair users, but for a child in a stroller, or anyone carrying bulky packages. Many of the features built into these homes also added significantly to their resale value.

While laws exist—notably the Americans with Disabilities Act of 1990 and similar legislation nation by nation in Europe—to make sure public buildings are accessible, no equivalent code of standards has ever been passed for the private home. This may change with the "graying of America." According to the Bureau of the Census, people over eighty-five comprise the fastest growing segment of the population; by 2050 more than one out of four Americans will be over sixty-five, and more than the current one in five will be people with disabilities. And these people don't want to move. According to a recent survey, 85 percent of people older than sixty-five have no intentions of moving, and a good 80 percent of them have mobility impairments. However, that doesn't mean they have to live in a hostile environment. Accommodating a broad range of ability and age groups is at the heart of Universal Design. This allows people to remain independent and self-sufficient in their own homes, and is truly beneficial to the broadest range of people. The government advocates it so that they keep people with disabilities in the workforce and paying taxes, not drawing on federal care programs. Insurance companies support it so that they can turn those people who receive benefits into those who pay premiums. And, of course, families want it, too.

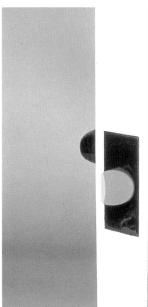

Access is in the details: Who wouldn't prefer a lever to a knob? One of the hallmarks of Universal Design is the switch to levers instead of doorknobs.

Your house changes, but you stay put, because it is designed to "grow with you." The movement toward "aging in place" has placed the

As the pieces of the puzzle come together in a home that follows the ideals of Universal Design, they complement one another. Here in Sands Point, NY, a wider door and lever handle work well with even parquet flooring to make the entry completely accessible.

emphasis, particularly strong in a market for 76 million baby boomers, on creating a home that will reflect the principles used to make public facilities accessible. Often they are one-story buildings, or those with a master bedroom downstairs near the living areas. The bathrooms and kitchens come loaded with an array of innovative ideas. These "greater later" houses are created for flexibility—supreme examples of planning ahead. Doorways and hallways are already wide enough for wheelchairs; kitchen cabinetry is adjustable in height for standing or sitting.

Seizing on this trend, Century 21 recently teamed with the Easter Seals to create an Easy Access Housing Design Award, an annual national competition for architects who build houses based on Universal Design. They use a checklist of criteria, mainly based on Ron Mace's work. There are well over 200 design enhancements in the repertoire of builders and architects who practice Universal Design, and more are devised every day. Here are just a few of the basics:

No steps. Entrance ways and the main floor should not only be level, but not have any sills or other "speed bumps." Not only will everyone enter and leave with greater ease, but think of what this does for moving furniture or heavy objects! Even a little job like clearing the snow on the path is that much less daunting when steps are not a consideration.

Wider hallways. While wheelchairs and walkers are the main motivation for this innovation, it is also a godsend for those carrying in many packages, or for big families passing each other countless times in the halls, scrambling to make it to school and work in the morning.

For safety's sake, the strong support of properly mounted handrails and grab bars and a nonslip, threshold-free floor minimize accidents in the most accident-prone of areas in the home: the bathroom.

Wider doors. This prevents scraping on narrow door frames, and is much easier when you are moving or carrying suitcases.

Levers in place of knobs. Hardly noticed, hardware can make all the difference for someone living with arthritis or another mobility impairment. A lever, as anyone who has tried to open a door with a bag of groceries in each hand can attest, is by far the easier way to open a door. Similarly, drawer pulls, windows, and plumbing fixtures should have levers rather than something that will make you turn or twist.

Technology-based solutions. In the second generation of Universal Design, particularly in the kitchen, levers have been replaced with push buttons or touch pads that activate hot and cold water or turn on the burners on a stove. Touch light switches, audible and visual smoke alarms, and power-operated doors and windows are also new innovations.

Nonslip floors. This innovation began with the bathroom and is becoming popular throughout the home. The introduction of low-pile carpeting, which is flatter and easier to navigate, makes this feasible.

Eliminating the often painful sills, rims, steps, edges, and curbs that made the old-fashioned bathroom a veritable obstacle course, the architects of Universal Design have devised a shower and bathroom that is completely on the level.

Showers and bath with no-step access. No more stubbed toes on sills or steps that are deceptively high. Studies have proven that there is less chance of slipping or falling when you can walk (or roll) straight in.

Roomier garages. Not only does a roomy garage make it easier to get in and out of the car, it is also big enough for a larger vehicle like a van. The first wheelchair-friendly vehicles were vans with lifts, and now of course the van and sports utility vehicle are the most popular rides on the road.

Elevators. Basements and upper levels should be designed to allow the addition of an elevator or stair lift. When mobility impairment is a factor, or develops, the remodeling involved in installing a stair lift is drastically reduced when the stairs are designed to be wide initially. Floor structures should also be planned to accept the later addition of an elevator. The cost of adapting an existing structure to add an in-home elevator is one of the greatest barriers to creating one—which might explain the popularity of unsightly wall-mounted stair lifts that are less safe. Architects can plan the shaftways and use the space for closets until the need for the elevator makes the conversion feasible.

Handrails and grab bars. Walls should be reinforced to accept rails and grab bars if they are needed in the future.

Light switches and touch pads. These should be placed low enough to be operated from a wheelchair or without reaching. Similarly breaker boxes, outlets, and appliances should be situated at heights that allow for greater ease of access. Many homes that embrace Universal Design use a laptop-style console or portable unit in each room to activate lights, curtains, doors, entertainment systems, and other appliances.

The principles of Universal Design have been codified in many ways since the time when Mace and his original team began their work. With the rapid pace of technological change in home design, it is almost impossible to create an exhaustive list of the latest and greatest features, but all follow the logic of the founders: Make it safe, make it easy, and look for the solution to the design problem while maintaining subtlety and beauty. What gives Universal Design tremendous integrity as a movement is a respect for the identity of people with disabilities as well as a concern for our needs as we age and our capabilities change. With each new generation of designers building upon the ideas of the last, taking ease and comfort to higher levels and utilizing the wonders of technology, the horizon for Universal Design becomes all the more vast.

1
Sheer Elegance

Elegance and Accessibility: A Show House

When Farmstead Hill Manor opened in June 1996, a show house for the best in regional design, one room in particular created a sensation both in the media and among the decorators who attended the exhibition. It was beautiful, no question; it was a dream room. But the real reason the luxurious, 18-by-23-foot library was featured on the network news was that it truly was a living room for all—the realization of the designer's intent to create an almost invisibly accessible, user-friendly space for people with varying abilities, without sacrificing style to function. Set in the historic Greenfield Hill section of Fairfield, Connecticut, the stately Georgian colonial, which showcased the work of twenty-one other designers, was open to the public as part of a benefit for Pegasus Therapeutic Riding, the Center for Independent Living of Southwestern Connecticut, and the Special Olympics. Inspired by these groups, interior designer Ron Marshall created a room that reflects not only his

Interior designer Ron Marshall created the sumptuous library, at left and above, of a decorator's show house to demonstrate just how beautifully barrier-free elements could be presented. The richly appointed room is proof positive that Universal Design makes no compromises when it comes to the degree of aesthetic satisfaction it offers.

Nothing could be more traditional in feel and in look than the butterscotch Brunschwig club chair. However, this chair is truly on the cutting edge of technology. A built-in lift helps those with mobility impairment, most often caused by knee and hip replacements, to rise with ease.

aesthetic standards—luxurious hominess—but addresses the realities of living with certain physical limitations.

Sumptuous furnishings, soft fabrics, and deft accessories established an atmosphere both plush and comfortable. Mahogany bookcases held rows of leather-bound classics to beckon the bibliophile; the soft sofas and chairs covered in green Ultrasuede and gold damask chenille invited visitors to sink into them and linger over a cup of tea or after-dinner glass of port. A linen tapestry print with a country motif adorned the pillows and window treatments. Could this opulent traditionalism really be an example of Universal Design and the home of the future?

As beauty meshed with practicality throughout the room, it was evident that the answer to this question was a resounding yes. In three seating areas, customized equipment for the wheelchair user and deaf resident was close at hand. Cozying up near the fireplace were two identical-looking butterscotch Brunschwig club chairs—handsome without being stuffy—but one had a secret built inside. Marshall and electronics expert Kim Michels had installed a hidden hydraulic lift in the chair, which could be accessed by remote control. The chair was designed so that at a touch of a button the cushion rose and tipped forward; while the chair remained stable, the person who wanted to stand was gently lifted.

The high-tech centerpiece of the room was a 9-by-14-inch remote-control touch-panel system that resembled a computer laptop. The programming panel controlled not only the TV, VCR, stereo, and lights, but could be preset to dial key phone numbers in case of an emergency, such as your physician or a next-door neighbor. The full range of high-tech services for people with disabilities was available in this single room. The television received closed captioning for the hearing impaired; there was also a TDD (telecommunication device for the deaf) set in a corner for easy use. Resembling a small typewriter, this device is hooked up to a monitor that displays both sides of a phone conversation.

Underlying it all was a flat Flemish tapestry rug, sisal mat, and a carpet with a pile low enough to ensure unimpeded mobility. "I test-drove a standard wheelchair on the carpet," says Marshall, "just to be sure." And the wheelchair itself? Marshall designed it, too. He integrated it harmoniously into the décor through color coordination and the addition of a throw pillow. He believes that there is no substitute for the look of classic chrome, although many wheelchair users do prefer lighter aluminum frames. "In my book, it deserves center stage, and that's where we placed it."

Ironically, it was this very detail that kept the room from being featured in leading architectural magazines at the time, although this view has changed as people with disabilities become more visible in the media. The dream library no longer exists—it came and went with the show house—but in its brief realization it proved many things. First, accessibility and beauty could be brought together in a way that completely minimizes and in some cases disguises the functional aspects of a room. Second, the technology exists to inconspicuously alter basic design elements, such as the club chairs, giving them a dual function: the chairs were not only aesthetically pleasing, but they fully accommodated a person with mobility impairment. Finally, this room decisively proved that Universal Design requires no sacrifices in the way of taste or comfort.

The décor is so elegant
and inviting, so full of the
luxurious appointments
of an English country house
library, that it takes
a moment before you spot
the chrome wheelchair, at
left, that is the only visible
indication of the need for
accessible design in the room.

Accessibility as an Art: The Rose Residence

One of the most tasteful and sophisticated homes in Avenel, a magnet for the social and political scene of the Capitol, is the Rose residence, opposite, where wide doorways and polished marble floors, above, offer smooth sailing for a wheelchair user.

Come on in to visit Michael and Carol Rose, entrepreneurs, major-league art collectors, and political insiders. Their recently built, 14,000-square-foot mansion is located in the most exclusive section of Potomac, Maryland, a community called Avenel that features meticulously landscaped re-creations of the English countryside, a professional tour-level golf course, and thoroughbred horse farms whose clean white fences border the main road. Most of the homes are overscaled, over-the-top Georgian Revival châteaux, but the Rose home is, by contrast, demurely proportioned and tasteful. It is also a model of up-to-date accessibility, since Michael Rose is a paraplegic and a wheelchair user.

Those are not the only ways in which the Rose residence differs from its neighbors. For one thing, it is a veritable museum, containing many of the greatest examples of contemporary Native American and Southwestern paintings and sculpture in private hands. The works, such as the virtuoso white Carrara marble

The brightly lit living room is graced by museum-quality works of contemporary Native American art, including marble sculptures by Larry Yazzie and Allen Houser, opposite, while the generously proportioned dining room, above, perfectly arranged for Michael Rose's wheelchair, is all the more comfortable for every guest thanks to the accessibility features.

sculpture by Allan Houser, a famous Chiricahua Apache artist, or paintings by Frank Howell and Oscar Namingha, are the focal points of most of the rooms in the home. Not only are the artists present through their work, but they are also frequently in residence as guests of the Roses, whose thirty-year marriage has been punctuated by numerous collecting forays to Santa Fe and other centers of Southwestern art.

Michael Rose knew all the strategies for designing a new house when he built his own place, his ninth home, from his experience as a professional builder of luxury homes. The home is custom-designed for a wheelchair user, yet beautifully wed to luxury. In addition to the gallerylike living room and foyer, the home has a cozy library, a billiards room, and an elevator. There is also the most marvelous entertainment center, complete with a movie theater; an old-time soda fountain and popcorn stand; and a vast gym, pool, and sauna.

The accessibility features are so perfectly concealed in the home that many guests are never quite aware of just how much has gone into the building to customize it for a wheelchair user. The three-part entry, designed in

While the eye is immediately drawn to the often humorous examples of contemporary art, above, the details of the Rose residence should not be missed: for example, the smooth stone surface of the floor, perfect for maneuvering a wheelchair; the abundance of light from the gracefully arched windows, allowing for complete visibility; or the ingenious, three-part, concealed ramped entry, below, that brings you to the front door while offering a glimpse into a room full of art treasures. Art is also the mainstay of the master bedroom, opposite.

accessible right-angled sections, does not feel like your typical, awkward ramp, but rather provides a scenic route to the front door. The stunning floor-to-ceiling windows and columns obscure the fact that all of the important living areas—living room, dining room, library, bathrooms, and master bedroom—are on one level. Visitors to the house remember the art, and that's just the way the Roses want it.

An architectural touch in the bedroom, the fireplace harmonizes with the manorial tone of the home. Above it, an extremely important portrait of *The General* by contemporary Native American artist J. D. Challenger.

Masterpiece of Modernism: The Schwartz House

The "wow" factor was not among the original principles codified by the founders of Universal Design, but it certainly is the dominant concept in the extraordinary home of Simeon and Nancy Schwartz in Petaluma, California. Starting with the splendor of the valley outspread below and culminating in the sheer grace of the glassy tower rising above, the home was, from the first sketches and ideas, created with access in mind. One of the children is a wheelchair user, and the marching orders for architects Chuck Peterson and Michael Rubenstein were to create an environment in which dignity and comfort could come together. The result is a virtuoso essay in modernism that takes Universal Design to a new height.

An elegant essay in the vocabulary of modernism, the Schwartz residence overlooking a cliff in Petaluma, CA is also completely fluent in the language of accessibility, designed to delight a young child who is a wheelchair user.

The operative metaphor of the design is that of a village amongst a grove of oak trees. To offer the children and adults excitement, comfort, and privacy, the character of the three linked buildings is individuated by color and form. As the architect Chuck

With echoes of the traditional Mission style of the region, and foreshadowing of the home of the future, the Schwartz residence combines the best of the past with the best of what is to come.

Light in all its glorious variety is the key to the visual appeal of the Schwartz home, whether it arrives tightly controlled by square windows along the elegantly curved stairs, above, or dances in a squiggle of neon above an arch, right, or simply floods a wall of glass bricks and cascades into the passageway between buildings, opposite.

The operative metaphor of the Schwartz plan is that of a village, an overall idea that holds together a group of connected buildings including the children's wing, opposite, which has the most extensive group of barrier-free features.

Peterson explains, "The curved walls and tall flat ceilings mark the entertainment and more public areas, while a pitched roof and simple rectilinear shapes define two separate bedroom spaces." For a dash of fun, a neon squiggle floats above a broken arch that announces your entrance to the children's wing.

This wing is where the accessibility features really come into play. Subtle but spacious exterior ramps and paths, as seen above, along with an elevator from the garage floor up to the first-floor bedroom area, allow a wheelchair user an easy path.

Making virtue of a necessity, grab bars used as bumpers and for exercise are painted green and accent the wide main hallway, which leads to a skylit rotunda. The rotunda, which allows easy access to each room and is spacious enough for a wheelchair to be able to pivot, also provides a marvelous infusion of light and a circulating breeze that is the hallmark of the house's design.

The dining room is protected from the strong coastal wind by pocket sliding glass doors that maintain the brilliant view of the valley. The knock-out vista is particularly wonderful in the living room, where the architects had a quandary: With a fireplace and a spectacular valley below, which becomes the focal point of the room? The solution was to install the fireplace within the curved glass walls of the tower, making it in effect a part of the view, and creating an almost sculptural effect of a cube within glass. The interior and exterior fireplace finish is smooth cement plaster coated with a faux glazing finish, as is the curved plaster hearth. It harmonizes beautifully with the glass surfaces as the colors wrap from the interior to the exterior.

The high-tech amenities that are particularly important for a child with disabilities are beautifully integrated into the workings of the house. An intercom system that is designed for hands-free use connects the village. Inside the bathrooms, sensor-controlled, hands-free faucets are among the conveniences. As one of the architects notes, "All of the complicated program and site requirements actually enhanced the aesthetic integrity of the project, creating a unique and fun experience living in the house."

Defying all the basic tenets that would dictate you can't have a fireplace and a panoramic view on the same wall, the architects found a way to build the hearth into a spectacular valley view, opposite, maintaining the sweep of the window's curve and effectively hiding away the chimney. In the bathroom, above, the openings below the sinks allow for a wheelchair user to get up close, and hands-free sensors turn on and off the water.

2

Right From the Start

New Homes and Building

For people with disabilities, creating a house that accommodates their specific needs has often meant spending hundreds of thousands of dollars for specialist architects and builders. Part of the problem lies in the exorbitant costs of remodeling, which involves working with a preexisting framework that has limitations. The larger part of the problem, and something that the Universal Design movement and this book is addressing, is that not enough architects and builders are anticipating the needs of an aging population, and integrating solutions that are already available into the design lexicon.

Universal Design is not something new that materialized with the passage of the Americans with Disabilities Act in 1990. It has an important precedent in architectural history: the work of the great Frank Lloyd Wright. While his homes could never be classified as the most comfortable places in which to live—notoriously cold and badly insulated, and bound to bruise even the shins

Rather than adapting an existing home, builders have found ways to incorporate the principles of Universal Design into new home construction, such as the wide double doors and a flush threshold between rooms, left, or the open spaces of the bedroom, above, in this Massachusetts home.

The light-filled dining room, opposite, deftly weaves beauty and barrier-free amenities in one economical package, while level access and ease of passage in a wheelchair are guaranteed by the open plan of the ground floor, above.

of the architect himself with the unconventional placement of low furniture—Frank Lloyd Wright's pure view of the interior is in many ways a fitting precursor to Universal Design. Wright believed in the same flow of movement from living space to kitchen and bedroom, and was similarly engaged in a pursuit of the simplicity that is at the core of Universal Design. Take, for example, the long low lines of the Robie House and other Prairie-style buildings. They are deliberately streamlined and simple, inside and out. The terms that Wright himself used were "swift" and "clean." Elaboration and unnecessary decoration were replaced with plain and utilitarian styles.

Another element of the Wright aesthetic that harmonizes perfectly with the tenets of accessibility was his addiction to light. "Let the modern now work with light, light

At the heart of the home is the kitchen, a gathering place for great ideas on accessibility as well as for guests. Shallow sinks, faucets with levers, well-lit and easily operated controls and adjustable countertops are harbingers of the Universal Design features that will, soon enough, be standard operating procedure in every new home.

Transforming a house into a barrier-free home begins with the simplest of additions: the ramp, above, that eliminates the dangers and difficulties of steps. In the cozy living room, right, clear spaces and snugly secured wall-to-wall carpeting allow for ease of movement for wheelchair users.

diffused, light reflected, light refracted—light for its own sake, shadows gratuitous," he wrote in his autobiography. For those with visual or hearing impairment—particularly people who have lost some of their hearing later in life and rely on lipreading to communicate—the need for good light throughout a room is particularly acute.

Wright's adherence to the idea of a home in which space flowed into space is particularly influential for the Universal Design movement. The physical realization of this freedom was the new feeling of space within the interior, which flowed from living area to dining area and beyond, removing the walls and corridors that created interior boxes. At his masterpiece, Fallingwater, the walls are sliding screens, with all the connotations of Japanese living. The extraordinary effect is even felt in the way sound travels through the building—the constant music of the stream pervades the structure.

The ideals of simplicity and repose, the elimination of the unnecessary, including interior walls and separate rooms, and the creation of what Wright called "spiritual integrity" within a home are not just limited to the grand houses, such as Robie House and Fallingwater. These ideas are also represented, albeit in different forms, in the latest wave of modular homes constructed with Universal Design features. By building these homes from scratch, the costs are remarkably low: Excluding land, the materials and construction for an average-sized home come to anywhere between $95,000 and $139,000.

The architectural plans emphasize accessibility and ease of movement, thanks in part to carpeting that is tightly secured and the wide open space that is reminiscent of Wright. The houses come equipped with 36-inch-wide swing doors, 42-inch-wide clearance in the hallways, low-pile carpeting, knee spaces with protection panels at kitchen appliances and bathrooms, sink faucets with push-pull lever handles, and audible and visual signals and alarms at the door. One of the first to benefit from the modular technique was a decorated Vietnam War veteran who is a wheelchair user. His home in Massachusetts is a model of the efficient, subtle achievement that is becoming renowned in the building world. The home has level walks and entrances in the front and back. The doors have lever handles. The electrical switches and controls are low and easily reached, and the windows are opened and closed electrically. The bathroom is state-of-the-art accessible.

As the Guggenheim Museum in New York was planned in January of 1944, its mastermind, Frank Lloyd Wright, wrote a letter to the Baroness Hilla Rebay, who was advising Solomon Guggenheim on the creation of the museum. His words now seem prophetic in retrospect: "The museum should be one extended, expansive, well-proportioned floor space from bottom to top—a wheelchair going around and up and down, throughout. No stops anywhere and such screened divisions of the space gloriously lit within from above as would deal appropriately with every group of paintings or individual paintings as you might want them classified. The atmosphere of the whole should be luminous from bright to dark—anywhere desired: a great calm and breadth pervading the whole place..."

When television reporter John Hockenberry was asked by the *New York Times* to pick a public building in New York that is, to him, the epitome of accessibility, he immediately seized on the graceful spiral of Wright's Guggenheim Museum. Conceived as one long pour of concrete, it is the ultimate ramp. Hockenberry mischievously fantasized about racing down it in his wheelchair. It is precisely this image, and the deeply held belief in the simplicity underlying it, that informs the origins of Universal Design. To understand what this design movement means for people with disabilities in particular, picture the graceful descent along that spiral and you will grasp its significance immediately.

Strong grab bars in the shower, installed at different heights, along with a hand-held showerhead, are among the essentials of the accessible bathroom, right.

3
Back to the Future

Historic Preservation and Universal Design: FDR's Top Cottage

A marvelous example of history and accessibility coming together is found at Franklin Delano Roosevelt's hideaway, Top Cottage, recently opened to the public. Long before the ADA, there was FDR. Although people did not know it at the time, he was breaking down barriers for people with disabilities with every historic move he made. While much of the legacy of Franklin Delano Roosevelt is known to lovers of history, one charming corner of the FDR story has come to light. In 1999, preservation architects put the finishing touches on an important project to restore Top Cottage and open it to the public as a National Parks Service site.

Up on a hill high over his home at Hyde Park in the Hudson Valley, just an hour or so north of Manhattan, Roosevelt created this writer's dream, a comfortable cottage situated with a breathtaking view of the Hudson River and the 20-mile length of the family compound where he and Eleanor lived. His plan was to retire and write

FDR at ease on the patio at Top Cottage, opposite, with a magnificent view of the Hudson in the background. Architectural historians call it the first example of accessible design to be planned by a person with a disability, and the president himself drew the initial sketch. He enjoys an informal moment with Winston Churchill and Mrs. W. Averill Harriman in June 1942, above.

his memoirs there in solitude. It never came to pass. For one thing, his possessive mother, Sarah Delano Roosevelt, made him swear never to spend the night there, so that he could be with her down at the main house at all hours. For another, his untimely death prevented him from realizing his dreams as a writer.

What excites the historians and architects at work on the project today is that Top Cottage was designed by Roosevelt. He even signed the architectural plans, much to the annoyance of the American Institute of Architects and Henry Toombs, an architect from Georgia, who was relegated to the role of associate on the project. It is the first house designed by a sitting president since Thomas Jefferson drew up the plans for Monticello. It is also, historians and architects contend, a great moment in history as the first house designed by a person with a disability for the prospect of independent living. Says preservation architect John Waite, in charge in restoring the Top Cottage, "He intended to live up there by himself, not having to depend on anyone, so that the whole cottage is centered on the idea of independent living long before that term gained popularity." As Allan Neumann, the president of Hudson River Heritage, points out, the exterior of the cottage reflects Roosevelt's delight in the Dutch-inspired vernacular architectural styles of the Hudson River Valley.

Built in 1938, and restored to its original splendor from 1945, the building is notable not only for its 360-degree view of the valley, but for its level entrances, ramps, numerous devices for easy living, and generous porch, which can be reached from the level of the living room. A highlight for FDR was the hearth, which he created so that he could roll right up and put a log on the fire or, in a turn that he found delicious, toast bread that he would butter and serve with a dollop of jam to guests. Says Allan Neumann, "What he wanted more than anything else was to create a relaxed atmosphere in which he served the guests, mixing their cocktails, barbecuing, making them feel at home, rather than have others do all of this." Among those who enjoyed the hospitality of Top Cottage were King George and Queen Elizabeth of England, who were treated to hot dogs grilled by FDR himself, and Winston Churchill, who sipped cocktails with the president. One of FDR's consorts, Dorothy Schiff, a reporter for the *New York Post*, built her retreat, The Red House, nearby, and the cottage was connected to it by carriage trails.

By today's standards, Top Cottage is not a state-of-the-art habitat. The door widths do not even meet the code of 32 inches—because FDR used wheelchairs that were nar-

row—they were actually dining- room chairs fitted with small wheels. But for its time it was an enormous breakthrough. The attitude of architect John Waite is model in itself. "We want to do more in the area of historic preservation and accessibility. Those who are interested in accessibility are too often blamed for defacing historic buildings, but we have worked out ways of making this a success, so that everybody can enjoy the building without disfiguring it, putting in clumsy ramps that call out that the people who use them are disabled. Our goal in historic preservation projects is having people go in the main doorway, not sneak in the back," he says.

A New Life for an Old Stable:
The Carroll Center for the Blind

A recent crop of buildings for the visually impaired has brought to architecture a revolutionary approach to the usage of light and contrast in design. The Carroll Center for the Blind in the Boston suburb of Newton is one such example. This former stable was a nineteenth-century structure that Graham Gund Architects transformed into classrooms, offices, and residences for about $700,000. Its renovation created a new environment that improves the lives of both the blind and sighted, just another example of the true universality of Universal Design.

The accent is on maneuverability and glare-free lighting at these renovated stables, where those with visual impairment share meals in the dining room, opposite, and gather in the common room, above. The architect of this project, Graham Gund, is acquainted with needs of the visually impaired firsthand. His brother, Gordon Gund, a major force in business and sports (he owns the Cleveland Cavaliers of the NBA), is blind.

There are many misconceptions regarding what "blind" means. Visual impairment does not always equate with a world of absolute darkness, any more than the hard of hearing live in a world of complete silence. For example, macular degeneration, a chronic disease that is the leading cause of blindness, gradually eliminates sight. Designers for the blind, grasping this important principle, now understand that an abundance of light is one of the first steps in making a successful building for the blind. In the Carroll Center, that light is created by a huge skylight in the central atrium and by windows throughout the building.

The next step for architects is to find a way to admit this light without glare, which is not only harmful but also disturbing to those with impaired sight. To that end, the abundant windows and skylights of the Carroll Center are created to pull in the right kind of light. Beginning in the central atrium, a trellis accentuates the form of the atrium for the sighted and filters the light for the visually impaired. The experience of the building is one of exploring the spokes that radiate from the central orientation area. Part of that process is auditory, and the building's high ceilings create a welcome acoustical space.

A variety of textures also provide sensory clues from which the visually impaired visitor pieces together the path that lies ahead. The process, called "wayfinding," is dependent on successful signals, such as the beginning of carpet against the end of tile or the texture of wood against stone, to give the person with a white cane a tactile indication of where he or she is located. Wayfinding also relies on the perception of contrast, and the Carroll Center relies strongly upon the juxtaposition of boldly contrasting colors to catch the limited vision of those who have some sight.

Another way in which the Carroll Center breaks new ground is in the "layering" of space. Small and large spaces, low and high, open and closed, hushed and busy, all serve in a complementary way with the contrast of materials to orient the individual who has some familiarity with the building, permitting him or her to build up a kind of "muscle memory" and sensory map. This is not unlike the way you can find your way to the bathroom in the middle of the night in a house or apartment that you have lived in for some time.

The Carroll Center embodies many of the latest innovations in building for the visually impaired, innovations that promote self-sufficiency and independence, such as wayfinding. With its empowering programs, such as mobility instruction and the low-vision clinic, and through its architecture, the mission of the founding director Father

The former horse stalls are perfect office areas, and the pattern of light and dark across the floor is ideal for "wayfinding," the use of the architectural rhythm of the building to guide one's steps.

Carroll is completely realized: "Our training must be such that we don't have to lean on it forever. It must be such that we can throw it aside and walk with new-found strength. It must be such that we are made, not dependent, but independent."

Within each of the stalls, a combination of available natural light and low-glare lamps is used to keep a diffused, glare-free space available to those with some vision. The textured floor is ideal for wayfinding with the use of a cane.

DBC
YLV
F   P
N   Z
O   C
H   E

The fundamental rule of design
for the visually impaired is the
use of contrast, as with the
juxtaposition of the dark carpet and the white dividing wall
and arch in this office area.
The open character of the
offices allows counselors to see
and guide their clients easily.

4

Toward Accessibility–
Room by Room

The Entry

The first test of accessibility in a home that adheres to a Universal Design is getting in and out. The step- and stair-free passage is one of the great contributions of this design philosophy to contemporary architecture.

The ideal entranceway is offered by a gently sloping walkway leading to a doorway without a sill. This is complemented by inconspicuous handrails on both sides for leverage and safety. The best rails are round or oval, although some designers prefer the feel of squared edges. The ideal height varies of course with the user, but most Universal Design consultants agree that between 33 and 36 inches is best. The optimum slope of the ramp is one inch for every 20 inches in length so that it does not look too conspicuous, and the ramp should be a minimum of 42 inches in width.

The aesthetics of ramps and walkways have evolved rapidly in the last five years. A major development was the use of

Farewell to tricky brick steps and flagstone paths. This gracefully curved, level, even path to both entrances of the Warren House in Woburn, MA, opposite and above, shows the way to the future.

If you can't get in the door, you can't call it home. At the house opposite and above, graded walkways to a threshold-free door make the approach easy. The path is more direct at the home at right, keying on the idea of level entry.

Even in a home as traditional as this family residence in Huntington Valley, PA, above, the subtle incorporation of a level path and entry can make the difference in accessibility. Where steps are inevitable, it is important to have features like a wide wraparound porch for easy wheeling around the house, opposite.

"switchbacks" or turns to break the length of the ramp into stages negotiable by a wheelchair (see the Rose Residence, page 9). Another elegant solution is the L-shaped, partly concealed (by a low wall) ramp that approaches the door from the side.

Since we do not live in an ideal world, steps are often unavoidable. When they must be used they should be low, broad, and made of nonslip materials. The surrounding areas should be well-lit. Every insurance statistic in history has pointed to the high accident rates of outdoor steps (along with slip-and-fall statistics in the bathroom) as the red flag of poor house design. Smarter steps have handrails and low-risers, as in the residence on the opposite page.

Once inside the entry, an even, spacious floor area, without scatter rugs or an obstacle course of tables, chairs, and bric-a-brac, is the key to ease of access. Generous lighting and open doorways clear the way for everyone to come on in and feel right at home.

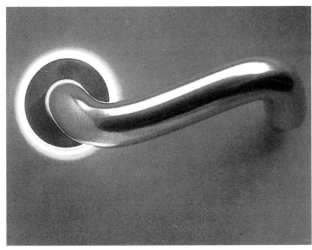

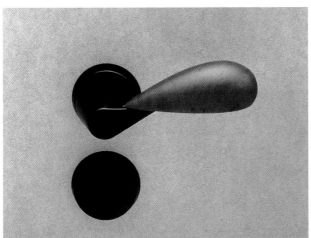

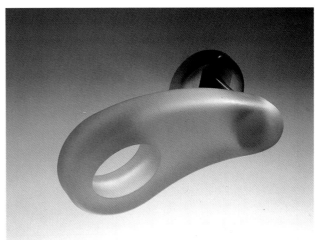

Once inside, it is impossible to over-state the importance of having plenty of room for a wide door, space in which a wheelchair can turn, and level transitions from the entryway to the rooms, opposite. This page, clockwise from upper left, variations on the theme of the lever handle: the Quaver; the push-round; the LUDUS; the P.S. 1; and the TACTA.

The Living Room

The yearning for wide open spaces is a natural impulse, certainly preceding the Universal Design movement, but the importance of having this extra space is now more than ever apparent. Wheelchairs need a minimum of five feet in which to turn; people with walkers or crutches also need a more generous passageway than most. However, as Universal Design changes have proven time and time again, these improvements also help other "hidden" segments of the population. When Universal Design pioneers reconfigured the turnstiles in the subways, the move proved most popular among pregnant women and mothers with baby carriages—an early indication of how smart design benefits many more people than its originally intended users.

Expanding on our natural yearning for more room for living, advocates of Universal Design strive for an opening up of bare floors, as you find at the home in Columbia, MO, opposite. The ideal flow from one living space to another envisioned by Frank Lloyd Wright is realized in the connected kitchen and living room of the Warren House in Woburn, MA, above.

Within a generous living space, it is important to provide chairs that are easy to get into and out of—not chairs that are low, or require twisting and bending motions. Push-up devices in the seat, whether hydraulic or electronic, make it much easier to get to your feet (see "Elegance and Accessibility: A Show House," page 4). A safe floor covering

By opening up broad aisles and using low-pile, wall-to-wall carpet, the Riverbank Center in Danvers, MA creates a room that is easy for all to use.

In this living room designed by Charles W. Moore Associates, above and opposite, a more generous separation of sofa and armchairs allow adequate space for maneuvering for those with mobility or visual impairment. The owner, who is blind, is able to tell he is in the living room as opposed to the hallway by the contrasting textures of the floor and by auditory clues. The living room floor, which has rugs centered on hardwood floorboards, resonates differently than the hallway, which is paved in tile.

is essential, whether low-pile, flat wall-to-wall carpeting, or taped down rugs—never small slippery throw rugs or area rugs. Psychologists point out that carpets with vibrant, colored patterns may be confusing for older and visually impaired people and recommend more soothing solid colors. Keeping any electric cords off the floors and out from underfoot is another important precaution.

For table lamps on end tables it is important to have controls or switches easily at hand, just as telephones must be within easy reach, with the large numbers that are back-lit for the sake of the visually impaired.

The top of the line in Universal Design is represented by full automation to the extent that a computer system, complete with timers, can open windows, draw the shades, and turn on lights according to a schedule, or enable the user to operate the windows and doors at the touch of a button. This same system can also control the thermostat and air-conditioning. However, from the opulence of the Connecticut show house to the everyday beauty of modular homes, these living rooms can still incorporate practical necessities with up-to-date interior design.

The Bathroom

A crowd numbering in the thousands has poured into the Cooper-Hewitt National Design Museum for the evening opening of the first important exhibition devoted to Universal Design in New York, and even before the show officially opens there is a crowd bottleneck: The state-of-the-art accessible bathroom has stopped them in their tracks. Although only a prototype, the brainchild of industrial designer Gianfranco Zaccai, it offers enough gleaming chrome and brilliant ideas to set the comfort-hungry in the burgeoning crowd dreaming. Over and over one hears the simple statement, "I want that."

Moving toward the ideals of Universal Design, this bathroom, opposite, in Chestnut Hill, MA uses an open floor plan, with more than the required 40-inch turning area needed for the radius of the average wheelchair, while the pioneering Otto Bock shower area offers a chair and hand-held shower with no step or metal lip to negotiate.

Perhaps it is the deceptively simple notion of a legless chair that glides across a hydraulic rail system situated in a wide-open shower area. Reached easily by a shower wand on a hose, the chair transforms the shower. Or perhaps it is the step-free entry into the shower, with no obstacles upon which to stub a toe or bang a shin. This shower-spa arrangement, separated from the rest of the bathroom by

State-of-the-art bathroom accessibility is found at this home in Sands Point, NY, where a level entry leads to a toilet with grab bars and a sink adjusted to wheelchair height, opposite. Above, the same bathroom also boasts a roll-in shower area and a bathtub with a removable side wall for an easy transfer from wheelchair to seat.

a curtain, is more spacious and safe. The stainless-steel grab bars are square and elegant, rather than the institutional round steel found in hospitals. Grab bars, in designer colors rather than steel and fitted with nylon grips instead of slippery metal, are also placed near the toilet and the tub to aid in entering and leaving the room.

A child could operate the adjustable sink and mirror unit, which rises and falls at the push of a button, and in fact that is the idea—that children, wheelchair users, and grandparents all find the height that is perfect for each of them. Horizontal adjust-

As simple as it seems, one of the great innovations of Universal Design is the shower seat, designed by HEWI, above. Among the design and engineering improvements to the bathroom are, clockwise from upper left, opposite page, the shallow sink by Kohler; easy-grip Mentadent toothbrushes; the Kohler bath and whirlpool with side door for wheelchair transfer; a fold-up seat for the shower by HEWI; ADA-compliant grab bars and hand-held showerhead by Alsons; and the touchless automatic faucet by Kohler.

ment is also possible, particularly useful in a bathroom where two people are trying to get to the train in the morning. The single lever faucet is one way to go, although "third generation" Universal Design standards now recommend push-button controls.

Similarly the toilet seat in this "dream bathroom" is wall mounted, not floor mounted, and rises from 10 inches from the ground (the American standard) to 24 inches, ideal for transfer from most wheelchairs. Most important, it is adjustable to anything in between. The toilet can also fold back into the wall and clean itself, an innovation that is simply brilliant. It will now be possible to put a toilet in the bedroom and not have a socially unacceptable bathroom gadget standing there all the time in plain view.

This complete bathroom ensemble is a model of safety and ease, with a grab bar-equipped tub and hand-held, roll-in shower with seat as well as level access all around and a lever rather than a doorknob on the door.

Reconfiguring the bath and shower for accessibility means rethinking the transfer board from wheelchair to tub and changing the height of a shower curtain for a roll-in, sit-down shower.

The bathtub at the Cooper-Hewitt is 17 inches deep, generous in its 30-by-60 inch dimensions, and made of a soft material. Water controls are push button for ease of use. A chair can be lowered hydraulically into the tub; transfer benches can also be used. A swivel chair that moves side to side and forward and back within the tub is another option, eliminating the old sensation of being fixed in one position for those who are mobility impaired.

The ideal accessible bathroom does not only have enough space—five feet across—but it has the ideal location. New homes in Sweden are, by code, required to have a full bathroom on the first floor, in anticipation of a population that, as it ages, will need to live on one floor. The typical 5-by-7-foot bathroom, ill-lit and badly ventilated, will not do in today's world. One elegant solution to this is the pocket door, or a door hinged to open into the hall rather than into the room. It is also a lifesaver when trying to help someone who has fallen or is in need of assistance, and the door width should be between 32 and 36 inches wide.

Although the ideal bathroom is symbolized by the prototype at the Cooper-Hewitt and located on the first floor of the home, many bathroom improvements—grab bars; transfer benches; wall-mounted, legless chairs; pocket doors—are already available from product manufacturers. In the meantime, we can look to Sweden as a model for changes that are essential to bathroom design.

With a level entry and dual hand-held showerheads, opposite, this bathroom has a head start on accessibility. It's easy to add a chair to expedite the process of transferring from a wheelchair. The elegant, postmodern look of the Otto Bock Orthopedic Industry shower and bath, above, underscores its seamless functionality.

With plenty of floor space for a wheelchair to turn around and a generously proportioned roll-in shower, the Warren House is already a model of accessibility. What puts it in a higher category? The open space under the shallow sink, with insulated pipes to protect the knees of a wheelchair user who rolls up to it.

The Kitchen

This spectacular kitchen, opposite, located in Tiburon, CA, has more to offer than just a splendid cathedral ceiling with natural timbers. It is a paradigm for unobstructed wheelchair-friendly floor plans. Mary Jo Peterson's brilliant solution, above right, to the problem of kitchen inaccessibility—installing adjustable sinks and counters—gained widespread attention as part of the Universal Design Excellence Project.

When family and friends gather at home, follow the sounds of laughter and banter to the center of the action. Where else but in the kitchen do you expect to find everybody? And that is also where you will find some of the great innovations in Universal Design, transforming what used to be a veritable obstacle course in the past into a showcase of great design today. With cooks dashing from the oven to the counter as well as guests milling around with a glass of wine, keeping up the patter, the kitchen is the nucleus of the twenty-first–century home. The best of the new designs generally follow an L-shaped or U-shaped plan, keeping a free path of at least five feet wide for walkers or wheelchairs to pivot. Keeping that floor space clear for wheelchair users and others, especially in front of the refrigerator, stove, and cooktop, is essential. Garbage containers and tables should be moved out of the way, hung, or folded down from the wall.

The traditional "work triangle" of the kitchen—the traffic among the sink, cooktop, and refrigerator—is a focus of Universal Design. Reducing the distances between any two points of the triangle, and then making the shifting of containers from one to the other easier to negotiate, is the primary concern in kitchen design. The accent here is on less lifting and reaching. More countertop space is essential to help shift the ingredients from the refrigerator to the oven, stove, or microwave, allowing containers to be slid rather than carried. Getting to the appliances is also an important consideration. The oven, cooktop, and dishwasher should be placed so that, for someone who has suffered a stroke and is no longer right-handed, for example, the approach from the left, right, or front is equally easy.

Tradition has it that one stands and cooks or cleans. What if I want to sit down? What if I am sitting in a wheelchair? That is the premise behind a new line of cooktops, installed at 30 or 32 inches high that

Gaining access to the appliances is the name of the game in the Warren House, above, where the oven and cooktop are adjusted in height to accommodate the wheelchair user. DuPont's multilevel countertop, opposite, with no-spill lip and safety-minded, aesthetically memorable, curved edges is ideal for both wheelchair users and standees.

are adjustable and insulated on the underside for the protection of wheelchair users. The countertop has a lip to contain spills, something that benefits anyone who dislikes mopping floors—and who doesn't fall into that category? Controls are easy to use, often push button rather than dials that have to be turned, with automatic shutoff timers as a standard feature.

At General Electric, a team of
designers came up with "real
life design," which aims at
making a kitchen as easy to
use for a wheelchair user, a
grandmother using a walker, or
her 9-year-old grandchild, as it
is for a man who is 6 feet tall.
Note, for example, the new
placement of the oven, which
makes it accessible for all.

The Real Life Design kitchen uses stock cabinetry but varies the counter heights from 30 inches, perfect for the wheelchair user, to 45 inches, which benefits taller people, to the traditional 35 inches. Another important feature uses roll-out storage on a level that can be reached easily. A 9-inch toe kick allows more floor space for those using a wheel-chair or walker.

The Real Life Design kitchen has particularly savvy solutions; for example, allowing knee space under key work surfaces, such as the counter. The pull-out, heat-resistant work surface under the microwave is ideal for a seated cook. A cutout that holds a bowl makes one-handed mixing a snap.

A three-bin recycling center, right, fits beautifully into the corner beneath the microwave. The bins slide out, eliminating heavy lifting, and there is two-way access to them, from both the kitchen and the adjacent mud room. The cooktop, opposite, is set in a heat-proof tile counter, making it easy to slide pots from the smooth surface of the stove to the countertop. The tile backsplash behind the cooktop retracts when not in use. Halogen heat comes up instantly and radiant heat from traditional coils is also available. Underneath the cooktop, above, cabinet doors fold away for valuable knee space or a stool.

Another major innovation of the Real Life Design kitchen is open shelving. This helps not only the busy cook see ingredients easily on open shelves or behind glass, but the person with Alzheimer's who might have difficulty remembering where items are stored.

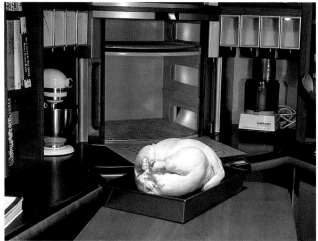

One important safety device is the magnetic induction cooktop that is not hot to the touch, and that uses a special type of stainless-steel cookware. The visual contrast between the hot surface and the counter helps in terms of safety. Throughout, the need for bright lighting is essential to help those who are visually impaired.

For appliances, location is paramount. Microwaves should be placed with plenty of counterspace nearby so hot dishes can be set down quickly. Refrigerators and freezers—many of them, dispersed in small drawerlike units—should be tucked underneath counters where they are most useful, with vegetables near a cutting board and meats over by the stove. Garbage disposals, installed near the back of the sink so there is knee space for wheelchairs,

Design history was made at the Rhode Island School of Design with the Kitchen Project, the world's most advanced Universal Design kitchen to date. It is composed of a "kit of parts" with interchangeable modular components for cooking, storing, preparing, and eating. The "Max" state is shown opposite, while the "Min" state is at left and right, above.

The Kitchen Project's compact, interchangeable components can be adjusted to fit the user in a "comfort zone," cutting counter clutter and making the most of non-interfering closures, no-spill edges, grab rails, and adjustable work heights and depth. A continuous "wet" surface that cleans as you work, point-source ventilation, recycling for water and waste, and adjustable carts for easy transfer and storage are some of the latest innovations in kitchen design.

Eliminating the need to reach and lift is the target of new storage systems that use rolling and sliding drawers, above and at right, to bring the dishes to you. The Amana cooktop is part of an ingenious new line of products for the older consumer that places controls up front and center rather than making the user reach across hot burners. Opposite, refrigerator drawers place items where they are most useful—by the counter.

In this GE kitchen, light comes from several sources, not just the window. Reflective surfaces and glare-free indirect lighting above the wall cabinets as well as cabinet lights in the cooktop area also provide additional light. Studies show that at age 60 we need three times more light than we did at age 20 to perform the same task. The lights in the kitchen are adjustable with sliding dimmer switches.

reduces the amount of garbage that has to be carried outside. Dishwashers should be located by the stove, where it is less noisy (older customers express displeasure with high noise levels) and easier. In the prototype of a "third generation" Universal Design kitchen, created by the Rhode Island School of Design (RISD) and unveiled at the Cooper-Hewitt National Museum of Design, there are pop-up dishwashers. Concealed in a console that tucks away at the push of a button, they use water recycled from cooking and are located just inches away from the range, allowing you to clean as you cook.

One of the forces for change in design has been the Paralyzed Veterans of America, a national organization that sponsors projects such as this kitchen, opposite. Note the wide-open space beneath the stove. Above, a design that incorporates the multi-level countertop idea into a center island.

The clutter-free countertops are echoed in the open floor plan of this kitchen. Note the fold-away doors that open to a knee space under the sink.

Get a grip: The revolution in utensil design began with the initiative to help those with arthritis or another type of chronic pain or loss of mobility. These utensils are equipped with extraordinary grips, such as the OXO Good Grips swivel peeler, above, or clockwise from upper left, opposite, the OXO kettle; the OXO Good Grips natural grip bread knife; the OXO Good Grips heavy-duty scrub brushes; the Copco chopper and bowl set; and the ETAC-RFSO rehab flatware set.

One of the most popular features of the RISD kitchen, accessible to children and wheelchair users alike, is the adjustable-height sink, which is available from some product manufacturers. In fact, the sink is placed in an adjustable countertop, and raised or lowered mechanically at the push of a button. For wheelchair users who tuck their knees under the sink, it is important to have a shallow basin, which provides more legroom and requires less reaching, and insulated pipes below to prevent getting burned.

The first generation of Universal Design introduced the single-lever faucet as an appliance that was easier to manipulate than turning a set of handles. Another major innovation was the use of the spray gun on a hose, allowing you to reach pots with the water rather than lifting and handling them. At this time, hot-water dispensers for tea and coffee, set at 190 degrees, were also introduced, saving the effort of putting on the kettle. Now the byword is touch pads and buttons to turn on and off the water, foregoing the need even to reach for a lever and pull. A panel of controls also opens cabinets and moves them down on adjustable height supports so that top shelves come into reach.

Inside those drawers, the gadgets and utensils are transformed by grip enhancers—soft rubber pull-on grips that make can openers and mixers that much easier to hold on to. A cutting board designed to be used with one hand, a pair of scissors that conforms to the shape of your hand and retains the memory of the shape, and nonslip mixing bowls are other new innovations. Uniformly lightweight and arranged inside cupboards on lazy Susans for easy access, these twenty-first–century implements make cooking a joy for all.

The Bedroom

Rethinking the bedroom for the twenty-first century is in many respects a matter of paying attention to details. Is there a large-numbered, back-lit telephone beside the bed? A ceiling heating panel for added warmth? What about an umbrella stand in the corner for canes and crutches? These are the sort of touches that can elevate a beautiful—if not entirely functional—bedroom of the 1980s into a living space and healing space for the next decade. It is, after all, not just a place to sleep, but a place in which one dresses, exercises, watches the tube, or reads or answers correspondence. This whole range of life activities requires a corresponding range of design ideas to keep pace.

Chairs in the room ought to have good, strong arms and firm, high seats—deep chairs that you sink into make it difficult to get up. Many armchairs are now fitted with automatic raising devices that are hydraulic or electronic (see page 4). Habitual readers ought

At the Zinder home, opposite, a spacious area of low-pile carpet around the bed and an elevator with level entry makes life easy for the wheelchair user. Above, the Paralyzed Veterans of America helped design this bedroom with a cozy fireplace and spacious floor plan, above.

to have good lighting, magnifying glasses, and book-holding as well as page-turning lecterns for easier handling, as well as a bed-reading pillow.

The bedroom is also a place to dress in, and closet design is of prime importance. A walk-in closet should also accommodate "rolling in," with room for a wheelchair or a walker. Automatic wardrobes, similar to a dry cleaner's, are another option. So are dressers or armoires with adjustable drawers that are fitted with easy-to-grasp C handles, not knobs.

If the bedroom is used for exercise, the floor covering is especially important. Wall-to-wall, low-pile carpet is much safer than area rugs. Good lighting, including night-lights in the hall and bedroom that are sensor activated or automatic, will prevent stumbles and disorientation. These are the improvements that transform a bedroom into a user-friendly area that is completely accessible.

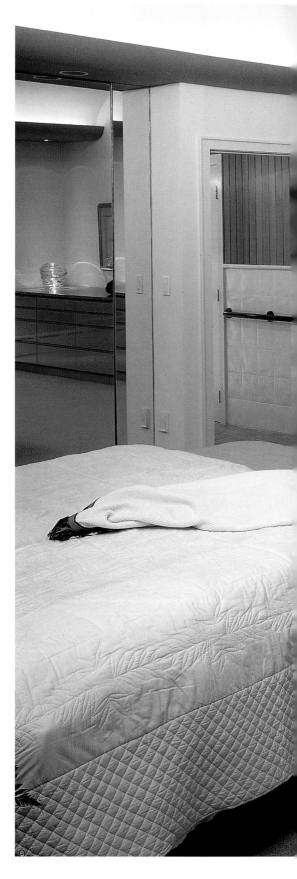

The path to the bathroom and hall is free and clear for the wheelchair user at the Zinder residence, where elegance and accessibility are deftly combined in one stunning interior.

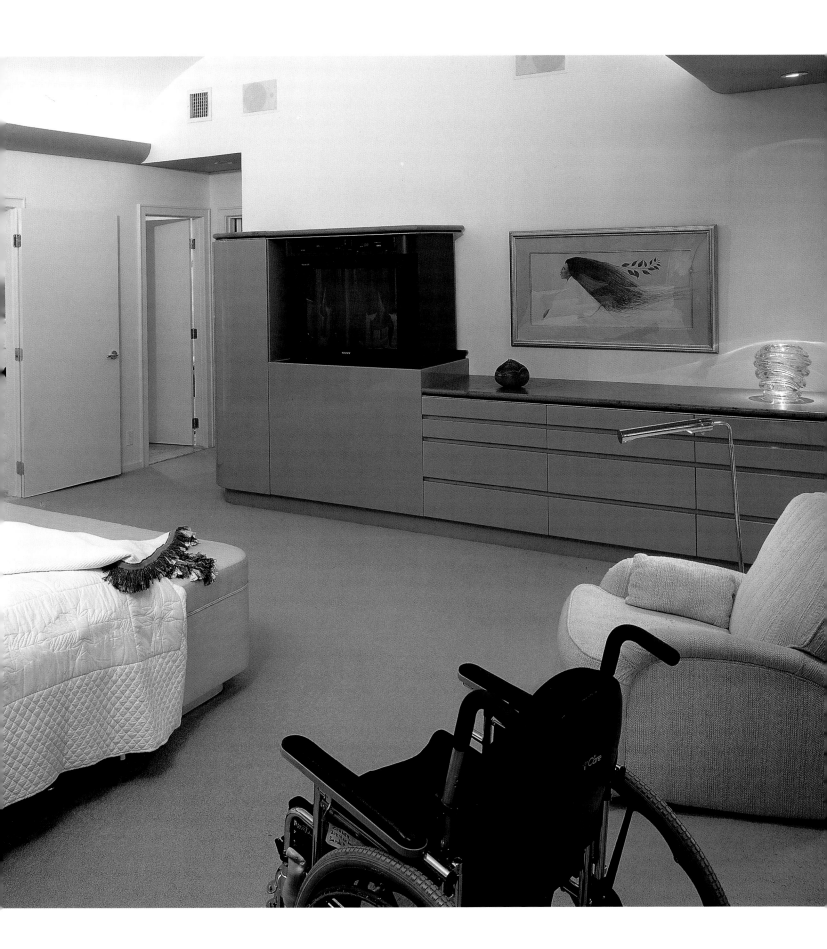

The Home Office

Even though corporate America is slowly recognizing people with disabilities as a largely over-looked pool of talent, it is still true that many who find it difficult to commute or gain access to conventional office spaces prefer to work at home. Nearly one-third of the 16 million people with disabilities with jobs maintain home offices, according to the National Organization on Disability. In this regard as in so many, they are on the cusp of a powerful trend toward electronic commuting and working at home. Although this was picked up by futurists nearly a decade ago, it is only now becoming feasible as our Internet and e-mail skills mature.

Not surprisingly, the core of the home office is the work station. First and foremost, the architecture of the desk and hardware must be accessible. However, the development of so many products—voice-activated computer software, new devices and programs for making computers respond to cues such as the blinking of

In the home office, where repetitive stress disorder is a concern, efficient design is good business and important for health. Opposite, the Steelcase chair and office system demand a minimum of effort for movement from computer to desk space and files. The Metaform table, above, by William Stumpf, allows for adjustable heights to accommodate all heights and seating arrangements.

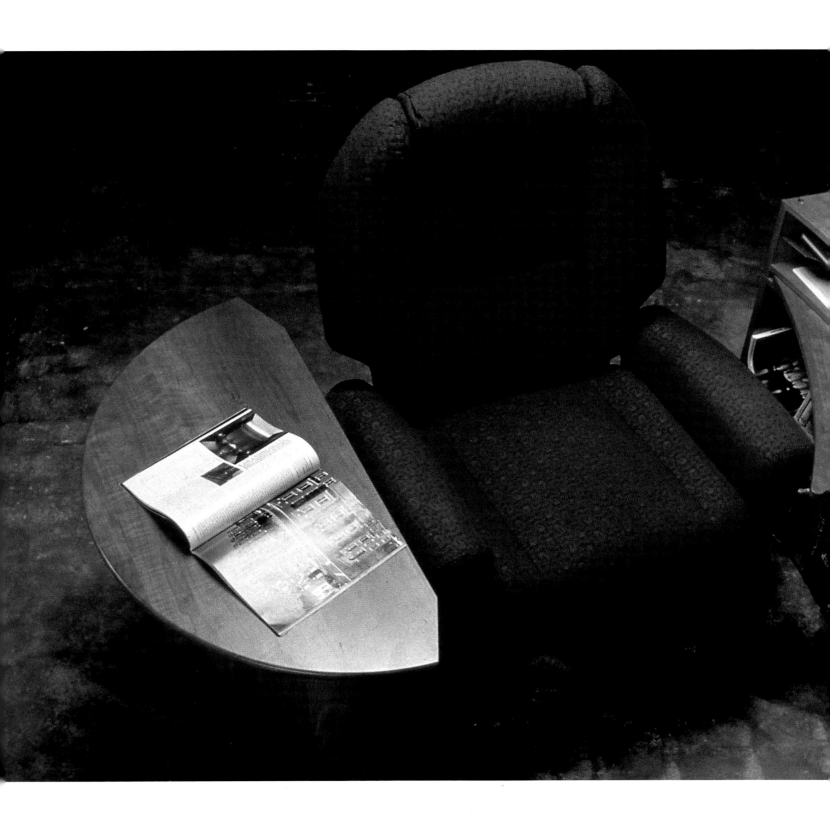

an eye or the nod of a head—make the prospect of working at home truly exciting. These endless possibilities for working at home were fantasies in the Massachusetts Institute of Technology's world-famous Media Lab just a few years ago.

The nation had a glimpse of what was possible when Christopher Reeve directed and starred in a remake of Alfred Hitchcock's *Rear Window*. During the film, Reeve used voice-activated programs, not only demonstrating how an architect could plan and design using the most basic and understandable of voice commands, but also how the villain could be caught when the system was used to open and lock doors, windows, and sound alarms.

Many of the world's top design firms, including Knoll and Steelcase as well as others, have turned their attention to the workstation and home office that incorporates Universal Design. Desks have been reconfigured; filing cabinets and storage systems are more flexible and mobile. Reaching and lifting are minimized, and so is the use of excessive paper. Many of the new gadgets are wonders, the result of major investments on behalf of corporations for research and development.

If the tools are the rules, as the shop-floor pundits say, then Pitney Bowes has set the standard for office machines with its brand-new, hot-off-the-prototype Universal Access Copier System. Name the disability, and this machine has the accessibility feature. For people with visual impairments, the 23-page-per-minute system incorporates advanced speech recognition technology, an extra-large, touch-screen interface, and Braille labeling on the control panel. To accommodate those in wheelchairs, the system has been designed lower to the ground than conventional office copiers and the angle of display can be adjusted.

The key to this copier is in the controls. Voice activation, touch screen, and the keyboard and keypad

This Metaform chair, table, and bookcase are the ergonomic brainchildren of William Stumpf and Associates. In one convenient unit, without the need to get up or reach, the tools you need for study or work are never far away.

Having been a design leader for decades, it is not unusual to find Knoll at the forefront of Universal Design as well. With the "parachute" chair, Knoll offers office furniture that moves with ease and can be quickly adjusted to suit the height and comfort of anyone.

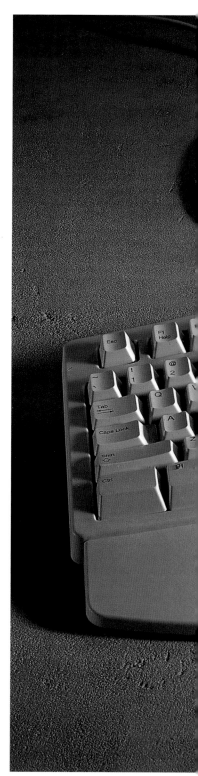

Addressing one of the most important disability-inducing problems of our time–repetitive stress disorder–Microsoft created the gracefully curved "Natural" keyboard, opposite. The Zelco Mouse Minder not only protects the computer mouse from damage but keeps it at hand, cutting time and energy.

interfaces allow users to choose the way they prefer to operate the system. Without even touching the copier, operators can adjust settings such as the number of copies, sorting, stapling, reductions, or enlargements. The copier will talk back to confirm the settings. The same choices can be made from a large touch-screen color monitor resting next to the machine. The size and location of the monitor are convenient for people using wheelchairs, and touch selections can be made with either a finger or a pointing stick. The copier control and control feeder are located at desk height, putting them within reach of operators in wheelchairs. This wonder machine, just one of many new instruments that are manifesting from the strong market for Universal Design, is something that will make the home office a reality. With the advent of more and more devices, it is going to be surprising to find anybody at headquarters in the future.

Credits

RIVERBANK CENTER, Danvers, MA
Architect
Steffian Bradley Associates, Inc.,
Boston, MA
Photography
Dimitri Papadimitriou, Medford,
MA; John Bellenis, Hamilton, MA
pages ii–iii; 66–67

SCHWARTZ HOME, Petaluma, CA
Architect
Chuck Peterson, AIA, and Michael
Rubenstein, AIA, Santa Rosa, CA
Photography
Tom Rider, Petaluma, CA
pages vi top left and right; xiii;
xvi–xvii; xxx–1; 16–27

SHOW HOUSE
Courtesy USAgency
Architect and Photography
AVISAMERICA
pages vi bottom; 28–39

CARROLL CENTER FOR THE BLIND,
Newton, MA
Architect
Graham Gund, Cambridge, MA
Photography
Steve Rosenthal, Concord, MA
pages vii top; 40–41; 46–47;
49–52

ZINDER RESIDENCE, Sands
Point, NY
Architect
Joshua Zinder, Cold Spring, NY
Photography
Mick Hales, Carmel, NY
pages vii center; xxii–xxiv; 72–73;
112; 114–15

KRUPP RESIDENCE, Huntington
Valley, PA
Architect
Joel Levinson Associates,
Philadelphia, PA
Photography
B+H Photographics,
Philadelphia, PA
pages vii bottom; 60; 62

FREEMAN RESIDENCE,
Chestnut Hill, MA
Architect
Hardaway Associates,
Newton, MA
Photography
John Horner, Belmont, MA
pages x; 70; 80

KWIKLIFT RESIDENTIAL ELEVATOR
Concord Elevator Inc.
Brampton, ON
Canada
page xiv

MAX AND MID KITCHEN
Installation Exhibit
Unlimited by Design
Cooper Hewitt National
Design Museum
Smithsonian Institution
Designer
Jane Langmuir
Rhode Island School of Design,
Providence, RI
pages xviii; 98–101

UNIVERSAL DESIGN EXCELLENCE
PROJECT
Architect
Ronald Mace, FAIA
Barrier Free Environments
Raleigh, NC
page xx

HEWI, INC., Lancaster, PA
Passage set, black, page xxi
Shower, page 74
Fold-up support and mirror,
page 75 bottom right
Bathtub, page 76
Shower stalls, pages 77; 79 bottom
Bath seat, page 78

WHITAKER-REINHEIMER
RESIDENCE, Berkeley, CA
Architect
Colleen Mahoney, AIA
Mahoney Associates, Tiburon, CA
Photography
Charles Callister Jr., North Bay, CA
pages xxvii; 61; 84

SHOW HOUSE
Designer
Ron Marshall, Fairfield, CT
Photography
Tim Lee, New Milford, CT
pages 2–4; 6–7

ROSE RESIDENCE, Potomac, MD
Architect
Chris Lessard, Vienna, VA
Photography
William Lebovich,
Chevy Chase, MD
pages 8–15

TOP COTTAGE, Hyde Park, NY
Architect
John G. Waite Associates
Photography
page 42 Daisy Stackley/FDR
Library; 43–45 FDR Library.
Hyde Park

NILES HOUSE, Clinton, CT
Architect
Arlene Tunney
Tunney Associates
Killingworth, CT
Photography
Robert Perron
Branford, CT
pages 54–55; 58 top; 59

WARREN HOUSE, Woburn, MA
Architect
Steffian Bradley Associates Inc.,
Boston, MA
Photography
Dimitri Papadimitriou,
Medford, MA
pages 56–57; 65; 82–83; 86

MAISANO HOUSE, Greenwich, CT
Architect
Edgewater Architects,
Old Greenwich, CT
Photography
Robert Perron, Branford, CT
pages 58 bottom; 107

QUAVER LEVER HANDLE
Modric Range, manufactured by
G. & S. Allgood Ltd. England
Designed by Alan Tye, RDI
page 63 top left
TACTA lever handle by Carlo
Bartoli
page 63, center left
LUDUS lever handle
Designed by Bonini Spicciolato

Manufactured by Columbo
Design, Italy
page 63 center right
P.S. 1 lever handle
Designed by Philippe Starck
page 63 bottom left
Made by F.S.B. Germany
—Courtesy The Ironmonger
   Inc., Chicago, IL

PUSH-ROUND handle by Lutz
Savant
page 63 top right

PEDEN RESIDENCE, Columbia, MO
Architect
Peckham + Wright Architects,
Columbia, MO
Photography
Deanna Dikeman, Columbia, MO
page 64

HOUSE NEAR NEW YORK
Architects
Charles W. Moore with
Richard B. Oliver, Charles W.
Moore Associates
now Centerbrook Architects
and Planners
Photography
Norman McGrath
New York, NY
pages 68–69

OTTO BOCK ORTHOPEDIC
INDUSTRY, INC., Minneapolis, MN
Shower, page 71
Bath, page 81

KOHLER
Bathroom sinks, page 75 top
and center left
Accessible bath, page 75 center
right

SHOWERHEAD AND GRAB BAR
Alsons Corporation
Hillsdale, MI
page 75 bottom left

BRUSHES BY MENTADENT
page 75 top right

GENERAL ELECTRIC KITCHENS
Louisville, KY
pages 88–89; 104–5
*Universal Design Excellence
Project*
Designer
Mary Jo Peterson
Kitchen sink, page 85
Real Life Design Kitchen
Designer
Mary Jo Peterson
pages 90–97

MULTI-LEVEL KITCHEN COUNTERS
Designer
DuPont Corian®
Photography
Barry Halkin
Courtesy DuPont Corian®
page 87

ROLLING STORAGE SYSTEM
AND KITCHEN
Architect
Paralyzed Veterans
Administration, Washington, D.C.
Photography
William Lebovich,
Chevy Chase, MD
pages 102 top; 106

STOVETOP AND REFRIGERATOR
DRAWERS
ProMatura Group, Oxford, MS
pages 102 lower left; 103

ROLLING COUNTER SPACE
Designer
Jane Langmuir, RISD
Photography
David Lund
page 102 lower right

KITCHEN
Access Remodeling Inc.,
Potomac, MD
**Consultant and Design/Build
Contractor**
Louis Tenenbaum
Designer
Alan Batson, AIA
Selection
Sue Ann Berlin Interior Design
Photography
Woody Cady, Bethesda, MD
pages 108–9

OXO KITCHEN PRODUCTS
Courtesy Smart Design
Good Grips swivel peeler,
page 110
Davin Stowell, Michael Callahan,
Tucker Viemeister, Dan Formosa,
Smart Design
Photography by Helena Fierlinger
Tea Kettles, page 111 top left
Vanessa Sica, Mari Ando, Scott
Bolden, Smart Design

Photography by Claus NY, Inc.
P. Medilek
*Good Grips natural grip bread
knife,* page 111 upper right
Scott Henderson, Smart Design
Photography by Claus NY, Inc.
P. Medilek
*Good Grips heavy-duty scrub
brushes,* page 111 center right
David Farrage, Smart Design
Photography by Claus NY, Inc.
P. Medilek

COPCO CHOPPER AND BOWL SET
page 111 lower right
Courtesy Smart Design
Annie Brekenfeld, Smart Design
Photography by Smart Design

CUTLERY
ETAC-RFSO rehab,
Waukesha, WI
page 111 lower left

CAUFIELD RESIDENCE
Architect
Paralyzed Veterans of America,
Washington, D.C.
Photography
William Lebovich,
Chevy Chase, MD
page 113

STEELCASE CHAIRS AND OFFICE
SYSTEM, Steelcase, Inc.,
Grand Rapids, MI
page 116

METAFORM CHAIR, TABLE,
& BOOKCASE
Designer
William Stumpf & Associates for
Herman Miller, Minneapolis, MN
pages 117–19

PARACHUTE GROUP
Designer
The Knoll Group, New York, NY
pages 120–1

MOUSE MINDER
Designer
Noel Zeller/Zelco,
Mount Vernon, NY
page 122

NATURAL KEYBOARD
Microsoft, Redmond, WA
Designer
Ziba Design
Photography
Michael Jones
pages 122–23

Resources

Organizations

EASTER SEALS
National Headquarters
230 West Monroe Street,
Ste. 1800
Chicago, IL 60606-4802
312/726-6200
312/726-4258 (TDD)
312/726-1494 (fax)
www.easter-seals.org
Non-profit, community-based health
agency helping people with disabilities
gain greater independence. Co-spon-
sors of the Easy Access Housing
Design Awards program.

THE CENTER FOR UNIVERSAL DESIGN
North Carolina State University
School of Design
Campus Box 8616
Raleigh, NC 27695-8613
919/515-3082
1-800-647-6777
919/515-3023 (fax)
www.design.ncsu.edu/cud
National research, information, and
technical assistance center that evalu-
ates, develops, and promotes accessible
and universal design in buildings and
related products.

CENTER FOR INCLUSIVE DESIGN &
ENVIROMENTAL ACCESS (IDEA)
School of Architecture and Planning
SUNY University at Buffalo
378 Hayes Hall
Buffalo, NY 14214
716/829-3485, ext. 329
716/645-2616 (TTY)
716/829-3861 (fax)
www.ap.buffalo.edu/~idea/
Provides resources and technical
expertise in architecture, product
design, facilities management, and the
social and behavioral sciences to fur-
ther the agenda of universal design.

CENTER FOR REHABILITATION
TECHNOLOGY
College of Architecture
Georgia Institute of Technology
490 10th Street
Atlanta, GA 30332-0156
404/894-4960
1-800-426-4833 (TTY)
404/894-9320 (fax)
www.arch.gatech.edu/crt
Provides support to individuals of any
age with disability within the state of
Georgia and beyond through expert
services, research, design, technological development, information dissemi-
nation, and education.

TRACE CENTER AND
DEVELOPMENT CENTER
University of Wisconsin-Madison
5901 Research Park Boulevard
Madison, WI 53719-1252
608/262-6966
608/263-5408 (TTY)
608/262-8848 (fax)
www.trace.wisc.edu
Non-profit research center that focuses
on making off-the-shelf technologies
and systems like computers, the
Internet, and information kiosks more
accessible for everyone through universal design.

PARALYZED VETERANS OF AMERICA
ARCHITECTURE AND BARRIER-FREE
DESIGN PROGRAM
National Office
801 18th St. NW
Washington, D.C. 20006
202/872-1300
1-800-424-8200
1-800-795-4327 (TTY)
202/416-7647 (fax)
www.pva.org
Veterans service organization formed
after World War II to serve veterans
with spinal cord injury or disease.
Provides guidance for accessibility in
housing.

THE LIGHTHOUSE INC.
111 East 59th Street
New York, NY 10022-1202
212/821-9200
1-800-829-0500
212/829-0500 (fax)
212/821-9713 (TTY)
www.lighthouse.org
info@lighthouse.org (e-mail)
Provides vision rehabilitation for people of all ages who are blind or partially
sighted. Its Manhattan-based headquarters building was developed by a
coordinated design team to create a
new model and working laboratory of
accessibility. A special wayfinding system includes large print, tactile,
Braille, and talking signs. Also offers
universal design–related courses.

VISIONS
500 Greenwich St.
3rd Floor
New York, NY 10013-1313
212/625-1616
212/219-4078 (fax)
www.visionsvcb.org
Non-profit charitable rehabilitation
and social service agency promoting
the independence of blind and visually
impaired people in the New York area.

NEC FOUNDATION OF AMERICA
8 Corporate Center Drive
Melville, NY 11747-3112
516/753-7021
516/753-7096 (fax)
www.nec.com/company/foundation
Supports programs with national reach
and impact in science and technology
education, principally at the secondary
level, and/or assistive technology for
people with disabilities.

THE NATIONAL ENDOWMENT FOR THE ARTS
The Nancy Hanks Center
1100 Pennsylvania Avenue NW
Washington, D.C. 20506-0001
202/682-5400
http:/arts.endow.gov
Endeavors to make the arts fully accessible to people with disabilities as well as older adults and people living in institutions.

THE COOPER-HEWITT NATIONAL DESIGN MUSEUM
Smithsonian Institution
2 East 91st Street
New York, NY 10128-0669
212/849-8300
212/849-8401 (fax)
www.si.edu/ndm
Museum devoted exclusively to the study of historical and contemporary design.

PROMATURA
142-Highway 30
Oxford, MS 38655
601/234-0158
601/234-0288 (fax)
www.promatura.com
Research and development company that helps businesses market and develop universal design products used by the mature market.

AMERICAN NATIONAL STANDARDS INSTITUTE
11 West 42nd Street
New York, NY 10036
212/642-4900
212/398-0023 (fax)
www.ansi.org
Set national standards for accessible design.

NATIONAL REHABILITATION INFORMATION CENTER
1010 Wayne Avenue Ste. 800
Silver Spring, MD 20910-5633
1-800-346-2742
301/562-2401 (fax)
www.naric.com
naricinfo@kra.com (e-mail)
Provides referral services, customized database searches, and document delivery.

ABLEDATA
8455 Colesville Road, Ste. 935
Silver Spring, MD 20910
1-800-227-0216
www.abledata.com
Provides information on assistive technology and rehabilitation equipment available in the United States through a database. Covers items such as white canes, adaptive clothing, low-vision reading systems, and voice output programs. Each product record provides a detailed description of the item, complete company contact information, and distributor listings (where applicable).

ADAPTIVE ENVIRONMENTS CENTER INC.
374 Congress St., Ste. 301
Boston, MA 02210
617/695-1225 (voice/TTY)
www.adaptenv.org
Promotes accessibility as well as universal design through education programs, technical assistance, training, consulting, publications, and design advocacy.

AMERICAN ASSOCIATION OF RETIRED PERSONS (AARP)
601 E Street
Washington, D.C. 20049
202/434-2277
1-800-424-3410
202/434-6561 (TTY)
www.aarp.org
Non-profit organization that seeks to help older people remain independent and in charge of their lives as they age.

THE CPB/WGBH NATIONAL CENTER FOR ACCESSIBLE MEDIA
WGBH Educational Foundation
125 Western Avenue
Boston, MA 02134
617/492-9258 (voice/TTY)
617/782-2155 (fax)
www.wgbh.org/wgbh/pages/ncam
NCAM@wgbh.org (e-mail)
Research and development facility that works to make media accessible to underserved populations such as disabled persons, minority-language users, and people with low literacy skills.

CARING SOLUTIONS
50 West Big Beaver, Ste. 590
Liberty Center
Troy, MI 48084
248/524-3652
248/524-2905 (fax)
www.caringsolutions.com
Provides customized, creative solutions for barrier-free living at home and/or the office, from consultation to design to completion.

ACCESS REMODELING INC.
P.O. Box 60027
Potomac, MD 20859-0027
301/983-0131
301/983-9698 (fax)
Universal design specialists offering building, design, and consulting services.

Selected Universal Design Manufacturers

HEWI INC.
2851 Old Tree Drive
Lancaster, PA 17603
1-877-HEWI-INC (439-4462)
717/293-3270 (fax)
www.hewi.com
Manufactures architectural hardware for barrier-free living, including lever handles, pull handles, handrails, cabinet handles, bathroom accessories, and grab bars.

ACCESSIBLE DESIGNS ADJUSTABLE SYSTEMS
94 N. Columbus Rd.
Athens, OH 45701
740/593-5240
740/593-7155 (fax)
www.ad-as.com
Accessible products for the kitchen

AQUA BATH
921 Cherokee Ave.
Nashville, TN 37207
615/227-0017
615/227-9446
aquabath@bellsouth.net (e-mail)
Accessible products for the bathroom

AQUA GLASS CORP.
Industrial Park
Adamsville, TN 38310
901/632-0911
901/632-2524
www.aquaglass.com
Accessible products for the bathroom

ELKAY MANUFACTURING
2222 Camden Ct.
Oak Brook, IL 60521
630/574-8484
630/574-5012 (fax)
www.elkay.com
ADA-compliant sinks

KOHLER CO.
444 Highland Dr.
Kohler, WI 53044
920/457-4441
920/457-1271 (fax)
www.kohlerco.com
Accessible and ADA-compliant
bathroom products

ROHL
1559 Sunland Lane
Costa Mesa, CA 92626
714/557-1933
714/557-8635 (fax)
www.rohlhome.com
Accessible products for the bathroom
and kitchen

MAAX U.S.A.
1625 James T. Rogers Rd.
Valdosta, GA 31603
912/247-2364
912/247-4967 (fax)
www.maax.com
Accessible products for the bathroom

STERLING PLUMBING GROUP
2900 Golf Rd.
Rolling Meadows, IL 60008
847/734-1777
847/734-4767
www.sterlingplumbing.com
ADA-compliant products for the
bathroom

OTTO BOCK ORTHOPEDIC INDUSTRY, INC.
3000 Xenium Lane North
Plymouth, MN 55441
1-800-328-4058
1-800-962-2549
www.ottobockus.com
Features Linido line of accessible
bathroom products

GE APPLIANCES
Appliance Park
Louisville, KY 40225
GE Answer Center:
1-800-626-2000
www.ge.com
Features "Real Life Design," a series
of accessible kitchen products

LASCO
3255 E. Miraloma Ave.
Anaheim, CA 92806
1-800-877-0464
1-800-775-2726 (fax)
www.lascobathware.com
Offers the "Freedom Line" of barrier-
free showers

Index

Page numbers in *italics* indicate
illustrations.